# NEVER

## THE
# REDS

## The Ultimate
# NOTTINGHAM FOREST

## QUIZ BOOK

# RICHARD HARRISON

The History Press

First published 2016

The History Press
The Mill, Brimscombe Port
Stroud, Gloucestershire, GL5 2QG
www.thehistorypress.co.uk

British Library Cataloguing in Publication Data.
A catalogue record for this book is available from the British Library.

ISBN 978 0 7509 6826 3

Typesetting and origination by The History Press
Printed and bound by CPI Group (UK) Ltd

# Contents

# Foreword

## By Forest's double European Cup-winning captain,

### JOHN McGOVERN

Forest is one of the clubs in the Championship that's got a very proud history – 150 years – so 2015–16 has been a very important year regarding celebrating it. When the Italian patriot Garibaldi came to England, his rousing public speeches inspired Forest to adopt his red shirt as their colour – hence the Garibaldi Reds. They won the FA Cup in 1898 and won it again in 1959, so there's some great history and it's something to celebrate.

I was part of the most magnificent period in the 1970s and '80s under Brian Clough and Peter Taylor – the best in the business. Taylor would recruit players and Clough would motivate them and give them confidence. There's even been a movie about it – *I Believe in Miracles* – showing the extraordinary feat the team achieved in gaining promotion, winning the League at the first attempt, winning the European Cup at the first attempt, and then retaining it.

The European Cup was in this country seven years out of eight, courtesy of Liverpool, Nottingham Forest and Aston Villa. In my humble opinion, none of the present-day sides in the Premier League could have lived with us, Liverpool or Villa – we were just better sides. Does it appear in this country seven years out of eight now? No. If anyone doubts that, that's the biggest statistic you need.

Half the statistics that you hear are just absolutely meaningless; telling you how far somebody has run and extolling their virtues. Only if you're running in the right positions at the right time and are contributing to your side winning the game does it mean anything whatsoever. The only statistic the manager needs to know when the final whistle blows is are we one goal in front? 'Cos if we are, that'll do me.

It is a privilege to have such a great history and something to be particularly proud of. I hope you enjoy testing yourselves on it here, rekindling some memories and maybe learning something new.

*John McGovern, 2016*

# Introduction

If, like me, you've ever 'watched' an entire Forest away match on Ceefax, made a 200-mile round trip to watch a meaningless mid-week pre-season friendly in torrential rain, or shouted 'Two! Two! Two!' when we won a corner in a game you were listening to on the radio, then this book is for you. And if you don't even support Forest but have a vague recollection that we were quite good in the days when we seemed to be called Brian Clough's Nottingham Forest, then this book is for you too.

We certainly were good once – more than once, in fact, and one of the aims of this book is to recognise that there is much more to Forest than the glory years under Clough in the late 1970s and '80s. By the end of the First World War we had won a League, triumphed in an FA Cup Final and appeared in numerous semi-finals, posted record scores in two competitions, sailed off on tour to a far-flung continent and won a national tournament to mark the end of the war. If the years between the wars were relatively unsuccessful (though not uneventful), the next quarter century made up for them, with two promotions, a further FA Cup win (finishing with only nine fit men), a genuine challenge for the double at a time when it had only been won once in the twentieth century, and a couple of seasons of European football.

That said, by the time Clough came along Forest were treading water in Division 2 and showing no sign of making a serious bid to return to the top flight any time soon. When Clough's mate Peter Taylor joined him, the gentleman whose Foreword you eagerly turned to before reading these words said it was no longer a case of *whether* Forest would get promoted but *when*. But he couldn't have imagined the run of success that would follow and it's not without reason that the 2015 film and book about what have come to be known as 'the glory years' (1975–1980) used the word 'miracle' to describe it. Needless to say, there's plenty in here for those who want to recall the times when Wembley trips seemed to be an annual event and it was a genuine surprise if we lost at home.

But even those with the rosiest of red-tinted spectacles would accept that Champions of Europe is not Forest's natural place in the scheme of things. That we have fallen so far since those days only emphasises just how high we climbed. Forest fans are sometimes accused of living in the past, but the level of support we retain in the face of high ticket prices and a prolonged lack of success on the field shows admirable loyalty in a troublesome present and commitment to an uncertain future.

In the century and a half since some blokes in a pub decided to give this new-fangled football lark a try, Forest have been magnificent (irregularly), rather ordinary (a lot of the time), and spectacularly poor (mercifully rarely). But we have frequently been at the forefront of new developments in the game, we can probably claim more 'firsts' than just about any other club, and we have consistently been admired for both the attractiveness and the discipline of our play (notwithstanding occasional dishonourable exceptions in both cases). Add to that one of the best and most distinctive club crests and well over a century at an enviable riverside location and, for many of us, being a Red is as much about the whole of the club's rich history as it is the trophy-laden years. Well, almost.

So whether you are a long-suffering Forest obsessive or a chance passer-by who has casually plucked this book from a shelf, I hope, to borrow from Lord Reith, that you will be informed, educated and entertained. None of which remotely applies to the Hillsborough tragedy of 1989, when ninety-six people went to a football match and never came home. It is the only significant event in Forest's history that I have consciously omitted, as a light-hearted book such as this is not the place to discuss it.

Otherwise, I have tried to condense 150 years into thirty rounds of eleven questions, inevitably concentrating on the more modern eras that most fans will remember or at least know a bit about. Although the vast majority of the questions deal with the years from the 1959 FA Cup win onwards, the preceding hundred years or so are far too eventful to ignore, so the first few rounds take us from the club's foundation to that second FA Cup win.

A book like this will inevitably and rightly celebrate the outstanding successes Forest have enjoyed, but it's the bad times that make the good ones so much better and I have included plenty of reminders that, as mentioned, there is much more to Forest than the rewards we reaped for having the game's best-ever manager at the peak of his powers.

Where possible I have tried to check the facts and confirm the anecdotes in one or more of the various statistical histories of the club and its players. I am particularly indebted here to the late Ken Smales' *Forest: The First 125 Years* (Temple Printing) and its successor, *Nottingham Forest: The Official Statistical History* (Pineapple Books). The opinions expressed are, of course, my own, likewise any errors that may have crept in.

While Forest haven't always had a great team, I hope this book gives ample evidence that we will always be one of the game's great clubs.

Richard Harrison, 2016

# Acknowledgements

In publishing my first book about Forest, I am indebted to:

My late father and mother, for the love of Forest and of writing, respectively.

Dean Smith, for giving me a platform for my early writings on Forest in the *Blooming Forest* fanzine.

John Lawson, for the chance to become a regular contributor to the Forest match programme.

John's successors as Forest programme editor, Nick Richardson, George Solomon and Ashley Lambell, for their continued encouragement and support, and, in George's case, for putting me in touch with the Forest store and with John McGovern as I planned this book.

John McGovern for his Foreword. When you've lifted the European Cup twice you get asked to do this sort of thing rather a lot. I'm grateful for John's support and hope he feels I have done the club he served so well justice.

Nottingham Forest FC, the original Reds, for almost half a century of memories. The highs have been unimaginable and the lows unbearable, but on balance Forest owe me precisely nothing.

Stuart, my regular match day companion, for sharing many of the high spots and calamities of the last forty-odd years with me. May the Reds continue to cause us delight and despair for many years to come. Delight, preferably.

Lastly my thanks to you for reading this book. There are a lot of Forest books out there and you chose to buy/borrow/ pinch this one. I hope you feel it was worth it.

# Round

# I

# 'Through the seasons before us'

Forest are recognised as the third oldest English professional football club, though it is arguably the second oldest, as Stoke City (who usually claim this accolade) were the result of a merger and a renaming, rather than having an unbroken existence as one club. From the beginning, the Reds were at the forefront of numerous new developments as the sport gained in popularity. So, to kick us off, here are some facts about the club's pioneering days.

1   Notts County date back to 1862, but in which year were Forest founded, thus creating the world's oldest local rivalry in professional football?

2 Which hockey-like sport, still played to this day (mainly in Scotland and the north of England), did the club's founders play before giving this new-fangled football game a try?

3 Unsurprisingly, the decision to form a football club was taken in a pub, the hostelry in question being located on Shakespeare Street. What was the name of the pub at the time?

4 Why was the club named Nottingham Forest?

5 Who was the Reds' first ever captain? Pleasingly, during the club's 150th anniversary season, at least one supporter's shirt bore his name on the back.

6 Which legendary goal scorer, born in the year Forest were founded, also played for the city's cricket and rugby teams and wore walking shoes rather than football boots, which he believed impaired his speed?

7 In 1874, which Forest player cut down a pair of cricket pads to protect his legs and thus, wearing them outside his socks, invented the shin pad?

8 Which attacking formation, in common use from the late nineteenth century to the 1950s, was first promoted by the aforementioned inventor of shin pads?

9 What was used for the first time by a referee in a game between Forest and Sheffield Norfolk in 1878?

10 In 1878, we began our first ever FA-Cup campaign with a 3–1 win at Beeston Cricket Club. Who did we beat?

11 In 1885 Forest became the first English club to contest an FA Cup semi-final in Scotland when we travelled north for a replay after a 1–1 draw in Derby. Who were the opponents who beat us 3–0 in Edinburgh?

# 'Down through history'

Forest continued to play a prominent role in the game and by the end of the nineteenth century the Reds had earned both League and Cup honours.

The pioneering spirit continued into the new century, with records set that remain to this day and the club's influence even spreading overseas.

1 Which team, whose founders in 1886 included former Forest players Fred Beardsley and Morris Bates, was originally known as Dial Square and wear red to this day thanks to a gift from Forest of a set of kit and a ball?

2 What were used for the first time in a representative game between the North and the South at Forest's Town Ground in 1891?

3   On 17 January 1891, Sandy Higgins was initially
    declared unfit to play, but went on to score five
    times (the only instance of a Forest player doing so)
    in what is still the FA Cup's biggest ever away win.
    Who did we beat and by what score?

4   Which competition did Forest play in for three years,
    becoming its third and final champions in 1892
    before its clubs were welcomed into an expanded
    Football League?

5   In Forest's debut Football League season, 1892/93,
    who were our first opponents and who were the
    first team we beat?

6   Having previously reached the FA Cup semi-finals
    four times, Forest finally reached the final for the
    first time in 1898. Where was the game against
    Derby County played?

7   Who scored Forest's goals in the 3–1 win?

8   What was unusual about the official pre-match team
    photo, in which Forest posed with the trophy?

9   As one of the first football teams to tour abroad,
    Forest beat eight local teams (scoring 57 goals and
    conceding only 4) in which two countries in 1905?

10 Which prominent team in one of those countries changed its colours from blue and white to red in honour of the Reds?

11 Forest achieved the joint biggest home win in top-flight history on 21 April 1909, though it transpired the opponents' lethargy may have been due in part to their enthusiastic celebrations at a team-mate's wedding in the run-up to the match. Who were those opponents and what was the score?

# 'We will follow the Forest'

More silverware was soon followed by Forest's longest spell out of the top flight, but, then as now, things were seldom dull. Times were often hard, with the Reds struggling for form on the pitch and for survival off it. This is probably the least-known period of Forest's history, so don't be surprised if some of these questions catch you out.

I  The outbreak of the First World War in 1914 left many clubs in a precarious financial position. How much money did the Football League grant to help keep Forest going in 1915?

2   In 1919, Midlands/Yorkshire regional league winners Forest won a two-legged final against the Lancashire regional league winners to win the so-called Victory Shield. Who did we beat 1–0 on aggregate to become the English champions, thanks to Noah Burton's goal in the away leg?

3   In 1920/21, hard-up Forest sold the ground rights for a home FA Cup 3rd-round tie for £1,500. The game was drawn 1–1 and the replay was also played on the opponents' ground. Who were those opponents, who beat us 2–0 at the second attempt?

4   What was unusual about the penalty winger Harry Martin scored to equalise for Forest against Bolton Wanderers on Boxing Day 1924?

5  Which centre-half joined Forest for £50 from
Consett Celtic in 1927 and went on to gain
two England caps despite playing in Division 2
throughout a Forest career that took in almost
400 appearances and many years' service in various
capacities after he finished playing?

6  In March 1931 Forest played a representative national
eleven for the first time – and beat them 3–1 in their
own backyard. Which country did the defeated
eleven represent?

7  In the 1930s, consideration was given to hosting
which other sport at the City Ground as a means
of fundraising? A promoter offered the club a
guaranteed return, but supporters protested and
the FA rejected the idea.

8  In March 1934, Forest's Jimmy Barrington did
something in the 4–2 defeat at Bury that a young
David Beckham would become famous for in
August 1996 – what?

9   In 1937/38, we avoided relegation from Division 2 by
    two thousandths of a goal, sending down the team
    we visited on the final day in the process. We drew
    2–2, equalising five minutes from time, after
    which our opponents hit the bar. Who were the
    unfortunate team to go down that day?

10  Which team were Forest travelling to play in
    September 1939, only to turn back on hearing that
    war had been declared on the eve of the game?

11  Forest spent the princely sum of £75 to repair
    damage caused in May 1941 to the City Ground
    pitch by what?

# 'On to victory'

After the difficult years between the wars, the good times finally returned under Billy Walker. Our longest-serving manager took us from a brief sojourn in the third tier to winning the FA Cup as an established Division 1 team. He should surely be the next Forest legend to have a stand named after him.

1 Forest stormed to the Division 3 (S) title in 1950/51, losing only six of our forty-six games (five of them by a single goal) and setting several records on the way. Which divisional record for points and club records for total and individual goals scored did we set, and who was responsible for the latter?

2  In 1951, a Christmas Day crowd of 61,062 (the biggest ever for a Forest League match outside the top flight) saw the Reds draw 1–1 away, with the crowd for the 2–1 home win on Boxing Day taking the total attendance over the two days to more than 100,000. Who were our opponents?

3  In 1956/57, Forest were promoted back to Division 1 after an absence of thirty-two years. What was our biggest winning margin of the season, achieved on successive Saturdays in February at Port Vale and at home to Barnsley?

4  Our worst result that season was a 4–0 thrashing at home by Middlesbrough. Which striker, described in the programme as 'definitely one to keep an eye on for the future', scored a hat-trick and who was the Boro goalkeeper?

5  We won 4–0 away ourselves in the penultimate game
   of the season to clinch promotion in second place
   behind Leicester City. Who did we beat?

6  The biggest crowd ever to watch a Forest League
   game was 66,346 at Old Trafford in February 1958.
   What was the significance of that match that made
   so many people want to see it?

7  When Forest won the FA Cup in 1958/59, which
   non-League team gave us an almighty scare in the
   3rd round, taking a 2-goal lead before we scraped a
   draw, thanks to an own-goal and a penalty?

8  Roy Dwight was one of our scorers in the 2–1 win
   in the final against a Luton Town side including
   future Forest manager Allan Brown. Dwight was
   later carried off with a broken leg and, with no
   substitutes in those days, his ten team-mates held
   out heroically for over an hour to win the trophy.
   Who was our other scorer?

9 Every team that wins a cup at Wembley now does it after the game, but in 1959 Forest were the first team to do it – what?

10 Forest's Cup-winning captain Jack Burkitt and manager Billy Walker were both born in which small West Midlands market town?

11 As a result of winning the Cup, Forest played a two-legged friendly against the winners of the Scottish FA Cup early the following season. We lost 3–2 at home and drew 2–2 away against which team?

# 'Nottingham, Nottingham, Nottingham'

Nottingham – England's City of Football
and City of Sport – can boast the world's oldest
professional football derby match, even if the rivalry
between Notts County and Forest has tended to
be rather one-sided for more than half a century.
Notts fans hate Forest with a passion, but in modern
times at least Forest supporters have saved their
fiercest enmity for the other County at the far end
of Brian Clough Way and tend to look on Notts
as a less successful sibling. You'll hear cheers at
the City Ground if it's announced that Notts are
winning their match. The reverse seldom applies.

1 Forest's first recorded game was a friendly against Notts on 22 March 1866, which thus created the sport's longest-standing derby match. The result is variously recorded as a goalless draw and a 1–0 win for Forest. So confident of victory were County that they were content for Forest to have a numerical advantage. How many players did we have to Notts' eleven?

2 Which venue was at different times the permanent home ground of both County and Forest?

3 Which was the only season (it feels a little superfluous to add 'to date') in which both Nottingham teams finished in the country's top ten?

4 The Nottingham derby at the City Ground on 27 March 1909 saw brothers Jim and Albert play in goal for the Reds and the Magpies respectively. What was their surname?

5 Which author and playwright wrote about a Forest–County match in *English Journey*, in which he describes a tour of the country he made in 1933?

6 Forest have played seven 'home' games at Meadow Lane – one in 1946 when the City Ground was flooded and six in 1968 after the Main Stand fire. How many of those games did we win?

7 What was the last season in which County played in a higher division than Forest?

8 Which was the last season in which County finished above Forest in the League?

9 Which short-lived fanzine adapted the name of an Alan Sillitoe novel and covered both Nottingham teams?

10  In the last competitive match between the teams in
    2011, who wellied home a dramatic equaliser in the
    last minute of extra time to take the League Cup tie
    to a penalty shoot-out, which the Reds won 4–3?

11  Which Forest player donated £500 to the Magpies'
    survival fund in 2003?

# Round

# 6

# 'We're second in the League'

... and we should be at the top! In 1966/67, Johnny Carey's exciting Forest team had a genuine chance of winning the League championship and FA Cup 'double', a feat which had then only been achieved three times (and only once in the twentieth century). In the end, the Reds finished second in Division 1 to the Manchester United team of Best, Law, Charlton and co., and reached the semi-final of the FA Cup. For a provincial team with relatively modest resources to come so close was remarkable, so here's a whole round on what is still one of the best-loved teams in Forest's history.

1  Which trainer/coach joined Forest at the start of the season and, arguably, played the motivational 'nasty cop' to manager Johnny Carey's thoughtful 'nice cop'?

2  Which senior player handed over the captaincy to
   Terry Hennessey at the start of the season but was
   still an ever-present in all tournaments?

3  Which team visited the City Ground on the opening
   day of the season and became the only away team to
   win on Trentside all season?

4  Which squad player scored a hat-trick in the 4–1
   thrashing of eventual champions Manchester United
   in October 1966?

5  The three games it took to settle Forest's FA Cup
   5th Round tie drew a total attendance of more than
   126,000. Remarkably, our opponents were a 3rd
   Division club – which one?

6 A Forest team of manager Johnny Carey, celebrity supporter Ted Moult and players John Barnwell and Bobby McKinlay played Arsenal in the first ever episode of which TV sport and general knowledge quiz that season?

7 Which Everton defender's reportedly premeditated challenge on Joe Baker early in the FA Cup 6th round tie ended the Forest striker's season and, arguably, cost the Reds a trophy?

8 In that epic 3–2 win against Everton, who set up all three of hat-trick hero Ian Storey-Moore's goals (including a dramatic last-minute winner, headed home at the fourth attempt)?

9 Who scored Forest's goal in the 2–1 defeat to Tottenham in the FA Cup semi-final at Hillsborough?

10 Forest's highest attendances of the season were 47,510 for the Everton FA Cup tie and 47,188 for the League win against Leicester City. How many attendances of more than 40,000 did Forest attract to the City Ground over the course of the season?

11 Terry Hennessey came third in the voting for which award?

# 'Off! Off! Off!'

Contrary to the media stereotype, Forest had a
reputation for fine football and sportsmanship long
before Brian Clough came along. The downside
of this ethos is that often the team has seemed to
lack toughness and be overrun by more physical
opponents. While enjoying the traditional Forest
passing game, fans on Trentside always like a
player who gets stuck in. Sometimes, though,
an aggressive approach can go too far ...

I  Forest's longstanding reputation for fair play
was exemplified by an unusually long period
without a player being sent off. How many years
were there between George Pritty's dismissal
against Millwall and Sammy Chapman getting his
marching orders against Leeds United?

2 Forest had six players sent off in League matches in the 1970s – and one player was dismissed on no fewer than three of those occasions – who?

3 His fearsome tackling and 'Psycho' nickname notwithstanding, how many times was Stuart Pearce sent off in his twelve years as a Forest player?

4 In March 1994 which Forest striker, returning from a two-month injury absence against Bolton Wanderers, scored what turned out to be the winner and was sent off for an elbowing offence, all within half an hour of coming on as a substitute?

5 Forest had nine players dismissed in League matches in 1999/2000. One of those nine was the Reds' player-manager – who was he?

6 Against which team did Forest have five players sent off between September 1999 and March 2001?

7 Who is Forest's most dismissed player ever? (No, it isn't the answer to question 2 ... )

8 Who were Forest visiting in August 2001 when we had both Stern John and Matthieu Louis-Jean sent off, yet still managed to hold out for a 0–0 draw?

9 Which key Forest defender was harshly dismissed in the first leg of the Division 1 play-off semi-final against Sheffield United in 2003 and thus missed the second leg, which the Reds lost after conceding 4 goals for the only time that season?

10 In October 2009, which French midfielder scored the only goal of the game in injury time against Barnsley, jumped into the Trent End to celebrate his first Forest goal – and was promptly sent off for a second booking?

11 In which of Forest's play-off catastrophes did we only manage to draw 0–0, despite our opponents being reduced to ten men after just two minutes?

# 'We're going to Grimsby'

Sometimes whatever will be will be and we find that we just aren't good enough for the division we're in. From our own chants of 'Gillies out!' to the opposition supporters' taunts of 'Going down, going down, going down', here are some painful reminders of our more recent relegations. Sorry – there'll be a happier round along in a minute.

1  Apart from Forest being relegated from Division 1, why was the 1971/72 season about as bad as it could get for a Reds fan?

2  When Forest were relegated from the inaugural Premier League in 1992/93, we actually conceded fewer goals than third-placed Norwich City. Our problem was at the other end of the pitch. How many – or rather how few – goals did we manage to score in forty-two matches?

3  When Forest finished bottom of the Premier League
   for a second time in 1996/97, Kevin Campbell and
   Alf-Inge Håland were joint top scorers with how
   many goals each?

4  Which international goalkeeper made his only four
   League starts for Forest in the last four games of
   that season?

5  The sale of which two key players at the start of the
   1998/99 season was one of the reasons for Pierre
   van Hooijdonk's strike, which contributed so much
   to Forest's eventual relegation?

6 Forest finished 11 points from safety that season and, despite winning our last three matches, achieved our lowest points total since 3 points were awarded for a win. How many points did we manage to gain?

7 What blunder did new manager Ron Atkinson make before his first game in charge against Arsenal at the City Ground?

8 Who scored Forest's last goal in the Premier League to date in the 1–0 win against Leicester City on the last day of the 1998/99 season?

9 In 2004/05, Forest didn't win until the tenth match of the season at home to West Ham. Who curled in a dramatic injury-time winner in what was the club's first match after the death of Brian Clough?

10 Later that season, who was briefly in charge of the Reds between Joe Kinnear's resignation and the arrival of Gary Megson?

11 In April 2005, with relegation looking ever more likely, future Red Dexter Blackstock scored twice as his team won 3–0 at the City Ground, the Reds' heaviest home defeat of the season. Which club was he on loan with at the time?

**Round**

**9**

# 'Brian Clough and Peter Taylor!'

In 1975, Forest were in Division 2, going nowhere slowly, when a certain Brian Clough breezed into the City Ground. Eighteen months later, the football genius was joined by his trusty sidekick Peter Taylor and things would never be the same again, as Forest enjoyed unprecedented and unimaginable success with the game's best-ever managerial partnership at the height of their powers.

1  Who was Clough's first signing for Forest?

2  Who scored the first goal of Brian Clough's long reign as Forest manager in the FA Cup 3rd round replay win at Tottenham on 8 January 1975?

3  At which Wembley final did Taylor lead Forest out, after the Football League had refused permission for both Clough and Taylor to lead the team out?

4  What was the title of Taylor's 1980 autobiography which caused some friction with Clough when it was published?

5  If Clough was 'the shop window', what was Taylor, in Clough's summary of their partnership?

6  What did Taylor say there would be less of in Clough's life after the two went their separate ways? At the start of his first autobiography, Clough said Taylor was right.

7  A 2–0 defeat in Clough's final home League game confirmed Forest's relegation from the inaugural Premier League, but the occasion turned into a celebration of Clough that even the away fans joined in. Who were the visiting team that day in May 1993?

8 Who scored the last goal of Clough's reign in the 2–1 Premier League defeat at Ipswich on 8 May 1993?

9 What was the name of the 2005 stage play about Brian Clough, which starred former *The Bill* actor Colin Tarrant?

10 How much did Forest fans raise in just eighteen months to pay for the statue of Brian Clough, which was unveiled in Nottingham city centre in 2008?

11 What is the name of the annual charity fun run held in Clough's and Taylor's memory at Donington Park?

# 'And now you're gonna believe us'

…the Reds are going up! The traumas of our various relegations and play-off failures are dealt with elsewhere, but once in a while it all comes together and Forest either sprint or limp to automatic promotion. Here's a round on those rare seasons when, instead of trudging home disappointed after the final game, we stick around for a lap of honour and quietly wonder how many of the team that got us promoted will be able to hold their own at the higher level.

1 Who top-scored with 27 League goals when Forest won promotion from Division 2 in 1956/57?

2 We're often told Forest only just scraped promotion in 1976/77, but by how many goals would Bolton Wanderers have had to win their final match at Bristol Rovers to pip us to third place?

3 Which kit manufacturer provided Forest's shirts for the 1976/77 season?

4 In successive home games in the autumn of 1976, Forest achieved scores of 5–1, 6–1 and 5–2 against which three teams?

5 Jon Moore's own-goal gave us a vital victory in our final game of the 1976/77 season and led to an urban myth that he had been voted Forest's Player of the Year (Tony Woodcock actually won that accolade). Who was the unfortunate Moore playing for?

6 Which long-serving central defender was our only ever-present player in the 1993/94 promotion season, featuring in forty-six League games plus eleven in the League, FA and Anglo-Italian Cups?

7　That same season, which two legends scored Forest's three memorable goals as we came from two down at bottom club Peterborough United to win 3–2 and clinch promotion with two games to play?

8　Who managed the Reds to that promotion? The following year he became the only Forest manager to receive the League Managers' Association's Manager of the Year award.

9　Who scored a vital late goal to beat Reading in the penultimate game of the 1997/98 season and clinch promotion back to the Premier League?

10　Which young striker was given a surprise debut in the final game of that season, when the First Division trophy was presented to Forest at West Bromwich Albion?

11　In 1997/98, Pierre van Hooijdonk and Kevin Campbell became only Forest's third strike pairing to score over 20 League goals each in a season (after Wally Ardron and Tommy Capel in 1950/51 and Tommy Wilson and Roy Dwight in 1958/59). How many did they score?

## Round

## II

# 'You what?'

Some questions don't lend themselves to themed rounds. Some themed rounds don't lend themselves to only having eleven questions. So here's a first mixed bag of odds and ends that seemed too good to leave out.

1  The William Hill Sports Book of the Year for 2005 was written about, and by the son of, a member of the 1959 FA Cup-winning team. Who was the player and what was the book's title?

2  Which two Scottish teams did Forest beat on our way to winning the Anglo-Scottish Cup in 1976/77?

3  Which Forest manager was the first in British football to sell four players for fees of £100,000 or more?

4  John Robertson scored eight times in twenty-eight
   appearances for Scotland, but what was unusual
   about the call-up he received to an international
   training camp in 1974?

5  In November 1960, the first touch of the ball in the
   career of which Reds goalkeeping legend was to pick
   the ball out of his net after an own-goal?

6  In March 1990, who cheekily scored the only goal of
   the game against Manchester City after nodding the
   ball off goalkeeper Andy Dibble's outstretched hand?

7  What was unusual about Marlon Harewood's
   celebration when he scored the first goal of Paul
   Hart's reign as Forest manager against Sheffield
   United in August 2001?

8  Which brothers and Forest team-mates both scored in England's 13–2 thrashing of Ireland at Sunderland in 1899?

9  Which young goalkeeper's thirteen appearances for Forest included two Wembley finals in 1992?

10  On 27 December 1971, the TV news cameras came to Nottingham to see Alan Ball and his white boots make their debut for Arsenal, but which Red stole his thunder by scoring after a mazy solo run estimated at 74 yards?

11  Which 1950s Forest legend submitted an entry in the 1973 competition to design the current Forest badge?

# 'The best damn team in the land'

Most Reds fans would probably have been delighted with mid-table obscurity in 1977/78, Forest's first season in Division 1 for five years. But Brian Clough didn't deal in obscurity. On his sacking by Leeds United in 1974, Clough famously said he wanted to win the League 'better' than Revie's Leeds had just done, which Revie felt was impossible as his team had only lost four games. Four seasons later, Forest lost just three games (two of them by a single goal) to become the last first-time winners of the League title until Leicester City's win in 2015/16.

1 What was the score in Forest's first game back in the top flight, after which Bill Shankly popped into the Reds' dressing room and said the League was there to be won?

2 Who scored all the goals in a 4–0 thrashing of Ipswich Town on 4 October 1977, prompting the Trent End to chant 'Hang your boots up, Mickey Mills!', the veteran England defender having previously suggested Forest's good start to the season might not last?

3 After a Forest away game on 17 December 1977, *Match of the Day* commentator Barry Davies concluded that the home team had been 'buried in their own backyard by a team that has the hallmark of its creator, Brian Clough'. Which team had we just thrashed and by what score?

4 On which ground did Forest secure the Championship with four matches still to play?

5 How many points ahead of runners-up (and reigning European champions) Liverpool did we finish?

6 How many, or rather how few, goals did we concede in our forty-two matches?

7 How many clean sheets did Peter Shilton keep in his thirty-seven League games?

8 What was our goal difference in the League that season?

9  Forest became the first club to win a clean sweep of the various players' awards. Who was voted the PFA Player of the Year?

10  And who was the PFA's Young Player of the Year?

11  Who became Forest's only ever winner of the Football Writers' Footballer of the Year award and would have been ever-present in the League but for missing the final game at Liverpool to attend the award ceremony?

**Round**

# 13

# 'Running round Wembley with the Cup'

Just fourteen years after Brian Clough described his team as 'Wembley virgins', Forest had reached six League Cup Finals, winning four of them and becoming the first team to retain the trophy and the first to reach three successive finals. We'll gloss over the comedy defending that gave Wolves their winner in the 1980 final and the non-performance in our other final against Manchester United in 1992 and have a look at those four victories.

1 The 1977/78 League Cup Final replay win against Liverpool at Old Trafford was Forest's only major Cup Final victory achieved wearing a change kit instead of the traditional red shirt. What colours did we wear that day?

2 That season we became the first club to win the League and League Cup double. In John McGovern's absence, who skippered the Reds in the replay and received the trophy?

3 How many goals did Forest score in six games to reach the final?

4 The win at Old Trafford meant that which Forest goalkeeper, having become the youngest keeper to play in a Wembley final, won a major trophy before making his League debut?

5 How many times did Garry Birtles find the net in the 1979 final against Southampton?

6 Which corny 1979 film about a washed-up alcoholic ex-footballer used footage from that 1979 final to provide authentic action for a Wembley clash of 'The Saints' and 'Leicester Forest'?

7 Who top-scored in our 1988/89 League Cup campaign with 7 goals?

8 Who scored 4 goals in the 1988/89 quarter-final against QPR, even though his feat tends to be overlooked, as the game is remembered more for Brian Clough slapping a couple of fans who had come on to the pitch to celebrate at the end?

9 Which member of the team that beat Luton in 1989 was the first player to win both the English and the Irish League Cups?

10 On 11 February 1990, the kick-off of Forest's televised League Cup semi-final first leg against Coventry was delayed by extended live coverage of which significant event?

11 Who scored the only goal of the 1989/90 final against Oldham Athletic?

# 'We've won the Cup twice!'

Some people say it was easier to win the European Cup
before it was reorganised to favour rich clubs
from big cities and inaccurately renamed as the
'Champions' League'. They are wrong. These days you
can finish fourth in your League, lose your first three
European games and still be in with a chance. When
Forest won it you had to be either the European
champions or your country's champions to qualify;
every team you played were a country's champions
and if you lost a tie you were out, not rewarded
with a place in another European competition.
Oh, and Forest's first ever tie was against Liverpool,
the reigning European champions, with the away leg
second, so our European Cup adventure could have
ended without our even having to get our passports
and atlases out. If we hadn't been so good…

1 Who scored Forest's first ever European Cup goal against Liverpool in only his third game for the club?

2 In November 1978, what distinction did Gary Mills achieve when he came on as a substitute against AEK Athens?

3 Who scored with a collector's item diving header in the first leg of the semi-final against Cologne, having taken the decision to play just four days after the death of his brother in a road accident?

4 Who headed the winner against Malmö in 1979 in his first ever European game, but missed the final in 1980 with a serious injury, having scored three times in four matches to help Forest to the final?

5 The Munich triumph was the 63rd competitive match Forest played in the 1978/79 season. How many of those did we lose?

6 Which three-time winners of the trophy did Forest beat 2–1 on aggregate in the 1980 semi-final?

7 Who became the first player to play in European Cup finals for two different English teams when he was part of the Forest team that retained the trophy in 1980?

8 Which member of the Hamburg team we defeated to retain the trophy in 1980 was the reigning European Footballer of the Year?

9 What gaffe did ITV match commentator Brian Moore make when the final whistle blew in Madrid that year?

10 Brian Clough won his second European Cup with Forest after just five years at the club. How many years did it take Alex Ferguson to achieve the same feat with Manchester United?

11 When the finalists on an episode of BBC TV's quiz show *Pointless* were asked to name members of Forest's European Cup-winning sides, which three players were pointless answers, i.e. names that none of the 100 people asked could think of?

# Round

# 15

# 'We'll support you ever more!'

For years, the sound of the 'we'll support you ever more' chant towards the end of a match at the City Ground was the away fans' acceptance that their team no longer had any hope of getting anything out of the game. But you couldn't honestly put together a Forest quiz book without acknowledging that sometimes we're the fans wondering if things could possibly get any worse. So here, especially for any passing Derby or Notts fans, is a round about the kind of traumas that make the successes all the sweeter. And what's worse, you'll be able to remember most of them. Sorry …

1 At the end of the 1912/13 season and the start of the following season, what was the rather alarming club record of successive defeats Forest suffered?

2 What is Forest's record League defeat? It was inflicted in a Division 2 game in April 1937.

3 Between March and November 1995, Forest were the first team to put together an unbeaten run of twenty-five Premier League games, but when we finally lost it was in spectacular fashion. Who beat us and by what score?

4 In 1998/99, Forest went on a club record run without a League win. How many winless games did we suffer before we managed to win 1–0 at Everton?

5 In our very next game, who came off the bench to score 4 goals in the last ten minutes for Manchester United in the embarrassing 8–1 defeat that Reds manager Ron Atkinson referred to as a 'nine-goal thriller'?

6 Forest have reached the play-offs four times and each time it's ended in tears as we've lost over two legs in the semi-finals. Which four teams have we failed to beat, always traumatically and usually from a position of strength?

7 In both 2003/04 and 2011/12, Forest managed to go seven League games without so much as scoring a goal – who were the managers of those goal-shy teams?

8 What was unusual about Derby's second goal in their 4–2 victory over Forest at Pride Park in the 2003/04 season?

9 Which non-League team did a youthful Forest team suffer a humiliating 3–2 defeat against in the 2005/06 LDV Trophy?

10 Which two Conference South sides did Forest need replays to beat in FA Cup ties in 2005/06 and 2006/07?

11 Forest having survived the first of those ties, which club, languishing in the lower reaches of League 2 and beset with financial problems, dumped the Reds out of the Cup 3–0?

# Round

# 16

# 'To Europe,
to Europe'

There's more to Forest's adventures in Europe than
the two stars above the badge. In the 1960s we
twice played in the Fairs Cup, while in the 1980s we
were cheated out of a final and as recently as the
mid-1990s we were the last British club in Europe.

1 Who scored Forest's first ever goal in
European competition?

2 And who scored Forest's last goal in a European tie?

3 Which team, who Forest would memorably meet
again eighteen years later, were the opposition
for Jack Burkitt's testimonial match in 1961?

4 Which team were the visitors for a friendly match
to mark Forest's centenary in September 1965?

5　Who scored in both legs of Forest's 5–0 aggregate win against Eintracht Frankfurt in the 1st round of the 1967/68 Fairs Cup?

6　What was embarrassing about Forest's 2nd round exit from the 1967/68 Fairs Cup against FC Zurich?

7　In the 1983/84 UEFA Cup, the two legs of our 3rd round tie against Celtic were watched by a total crowd of more than 100,000. Who scored Forest's goals in the 2–1 win at Celtic that gave us victory by the same score on aggregate?

8　A notorious performance from a referee to whom, it turned out, a 'loan' of £18,000 had been paid by Forest's opponents, knocked the Reds out of the 1983/84 UEFA Cup semi-final, 3–2 on aggregate. Which was the club in question?

9 How many seasons of European competition did Forest miss out on because of the ban on all English clubs imposed as a result of Liverpool supporters' role in the 1985 Heysel Stadium disaster?

10 In which season were Forest most recently the last British team in European competition?

11 Who is the only Forest player to have scored in the European Cup, the Super Cup and the UEFA Cup?

# Round

# 17

# 'He's gonna cry in a minute'

Brian Clough's second great Forest side of the late 1980s and early '90s came very close to winning him the one trophy to elude him throughout his illustrious career, the FA Cup. Three times in four years Forest reached the semi-final, but our run of six Wembley finals in four seasons only included one in the biggest Cup of them all. The 1991 FA Cup Final was billed as Brian Clough versus Terry Venables, but in the end it was the antics of an adrenalin-fuelled opponent and a weak referee that had the most bearing on the destination of the trophy. It was a disappointing end to the Cup run, but in Nottingham the next day there was a hero's welcome for Clough and his team, with particular support for Des Walker, whose unfortunate own-goal in extra time ended up winning the Cup for Tottenham.

1 What was unusual about Forest's routes to the later stages of the Cup in 1988 and 1991?

2 Which winger, in his second spell with his hometown club, scored in the wins against Halifax and Orient in the 3rd and 4th rounds in 1988?

3 Paul Wilkinson and Brian Rice scored memorable goals in the 2–1 win at Arsenal in the 6th round in 1988, but whose passes set up both goals?

4 How many goals did Forest concede on our way to the 1989 semi-final?

5 Which Liverpool forward scored twice against Forest in both the 1988 and the replayed 1989 semi-finals, but is better remembered on Trentside for apparently mocking Brian Laws after his own-goal in the latter game?

6 Who scored Forest's goal in that replayed 1989 semi-final?

7 Who scored a hat-trick in our 3–1 win against Southampton in the 1991 5th round replay?

8 Which former Forest centre-half played for West Ham against the Reds in the 1991 semi-final?

9 What did the rosette Brian Clough wear on his Cup Final suit proclaim him to be?

10 Within the first fifteen minutes of the final, Paul Gascoigne committed two offences that would each have been given a red card these days, in the second of which he sustained a career-threatening cruciate ligament injury. Who were the Forest players he all but cut in two?

11 And who was the referee who didn't so much as book Gascoigne, later explaining this was due to his feeling sorry for the reckless Geordie?

# 'Psycho, Psycho, Psycho!'

Surely the most popular Forest player of all time,
Stuart Pearce deserves a round to himself. Saying he
would rather take his chances on the dole than be
employed by Derby County would be enough to make
him a legend on Trentside, but he also happens to
have made the third-highest number of appearances
for the club and is our eleventh-highest scorer of all
time – from left back! And the sight of him flexing
his biceps and roaring his commitment in front of
the Trent End before a match used to give many a
grown man a 'something in my eye' moment…

I  Pearce joined Forest from Coventry City as part
   of a double deal which saw which centre-half also
   arrive on Trentside?

2  In his early years at Forest, Pearce advertised his services in the match programme as what kind of tradesman?

3  In the 1990/91 season, Pearce got over the disappointments of Italia 90 to such an extent that many people feel he should have been named as Footballer of the Year instead of Leeds United's Gordon Strachan. How many goals did Pearce score (excluding penalties) from left-back that season?

4  What unusual Pearce-related souvenir was available from the Forest club shop in the early 1990s?

5  How many of his seventy-eight England caps did Pearce win as a Forest player?

6  In 1996, Forest won Pearce's testimonial match 6–5 in front of a crowd of 23,818 (the club's highest ever for a benefit match) and the kick-off had to be delayed while they took their places. Who was the game against? Their manager had told his players their season wasn't over until they had honoured Pearce.

7  What was wrong with the initial team Pearce selected for his first game as caretaker in charge of Forest against Arsenal in December 1996?

8  According to the lyrics of the 1998 version of 'Three Lions', what was Psycho doing?

9  What was Pearce's answer when asked to choose red sauce, brown sauce or no sauce at all in the Sausage Sandwich Game on Danny Baker's radio show?

10  The tumultuous reception he got from the fans
    made Pearce's first League game in charge of
    Forest in 2014 one of those 'I was there' moments –
    who did we play in that game?

11  In a much-quoted mixing of metaphors, what did
    Pearce once famously say he could see 'at the end of
    the tunnel'?

# Round
# 19

# 'He's one of our own'

Here's a half-decent team of players for you to identify – all were born within Robin Hood's county and all played for Forest in the last fifty years.

1  Which keeper played for all three Notts clubs, making a total of more than 400 League appearances for them, including nearly every game of Forest's play-off season of 2002/03?

2 Which Forest player – reportedly Sven-Göran Eriksson's favourite player in his day – was the first black player to play a full international for England, a feat referred to in the title of his autobiography, *First Among Unequals*?

3 In a bizarre game at Swindon in January 2008 – a 2–1 defeat in torrential rain, in which Forest players scored all three goals – which substitute managed to be booked without even taking the field, for mocking the home supporters when a shot stopped short in the mud, allowing one of his team-mates to clear what would have been a certain goal?

4 Who was the last player to make 500 or more competitive appearances for the Reds?

5 The erroneous use of which long-serving centre back's nickname as a Twitter handle led to an unsuspecting American becoming a Forest fan for life?

6 Which member of the team that came close to doing the double in 1966/67 played his last game for Forest on the day John Robertson made his debut?

7 Which speedy winger scored a hat-trick against Forest for Coventry in 1999 but helped the Reds reach the play-offs in a successful loan spell in 2003?

8   Who became the first teenager to be sold for a fee
    of £5 million when he joined Newcastle United in
    2002? He only played thirty-three games for the
    Reds before his move, but had already captained
    Forest at the tender age of 18.

9   Which striker was Brian Clough's regular squash
    opponent and made his breakthrough after the sale
    of Peter Withe and the failure of Steve Elliott to
    make an impression in the first team?

10  Which striker surprisingly left the European
    champions to try his luck in a foreign league when
    he left Nottingham for Cologne in 1979?

11  Which Red's autobiography is entitled *The Man With
    Maradona's Shirt*? He swapped the shirt in question for
    his own after the infamous 'hand of God' game, his
    miss-hit back-pass having given the Argentinian the
    opportunity to punch the ball into the England net.

# 'He scores when he wants'

The City Ground has sometimes been known as something of a strikers' graveyard over the years, with rather too many struggling to find the net while in the Garibaldi, only to rediscover their touch elsewhere. But we've had our share of impressive goal-scoring feats too, in individual games or over the course of a season or career. Here are some achievements of note from the last century or so.

1   Grenville Morris holds Forest's overall career record of goals scored in competitive matches. How many did he score between 1898 and 1913?

2   Which striker scored 4 goals in a match three times in two months in 1935?

3  In 1936/37, which Irish international scored in eight
successive League games on his way to setting what
was then the club's individual scoring record of 31
League and Cup goals?

4  We completed the double over eight teams in winning
the Division 3 (S) title in 1950/51. One of those
doubles was over Gillingham with an aggregate
score of 13–3 (9–2 and 4–1) – who scored hat-tricks
in both games?

5  In 1958/59, which player twice scored hat-tricks
in games at Leicester's Filbert Street, scoring all
the goals in a 3–0 League win and 3 of Forest's 5
in the FA Cup 5th-round second replay against
Birmingham City?

6  As well as being able to jump over a Mini and throw
   a golf ball the length of the City Ground pitch,
   Duncan McKenzie was a handy goal scorer –
   how many did he score in forty-one Division 2
   games in 1973/74, prompting a certain Brian Clough
   to buy him for Leeds United?

7  Who is the only Forest player to have scored the
   BBC's Goal of the Season?

8  Despite our victories in Munich and Madrid each being
   by a single goal, we have had five players on our
   books who scored in a final of either the European
   Cup or the Champions' League. Name the three
   who scored in finals for other teams.

9  Which two Forest players scored hat-tricks in the 6–2
   win at Chelsea in 1986/87? They were able to claim a
   match ball each, as the original ball went flat and was
   replaced during the game.

10  Who scored Forest's quickest-ever goal when he
    netted against Norwich City after just fourteen
    seconds in March 2000?

11  At the time of writing, who was the last Forest
    player to score 4 goals in a League match and the
    only one to achieve the feat away from home?

# Round

# 21

# 'You what? You what?'

Another round of odds and ends that don't quite
fit into the themed rounds but deserve to be
included somewhere: the quizzing equivalent,
perhaps, of a midfielder who regularly scores
goals but doesn't track back enough.

1 Over the years, four players have captained
England whilst Forest players. Name them.

2 Who scored Forest's goal in front of 90,000 at the
Nou Camp to help the Reds to a 1–1 draw and
a 2–1 aggregate victory over Barcelona in the
1980/81 European Super Cup?

3  Which Forest manager, born on the day we won the FA Cup in 1959, invited two disgruntled supporters into the dressing room to address the players after a particularly dismal 3–0 defeat at Yeovil in 2005?

4  Which two Forest players made it into Esso's commemorative coin collection for the 1970 World Cup in Mexico without either of them making the final squad?

5  It was nearly 'Hello, good evening and welcome' to a career on Trentside for which future TV satirist and interviewer, who had a trial with Forest as a young goalkeeper?

6  Which company became Forest's first shirt sponsor in 1981?

7 Which Forest player took a bite out of a supporter's hotdog after running over to join the fans' celebrations when he scored at Blackpool in October 2012?

8 On two occasions, four players from Brian Clough's second great Forest team were included in an England starting eleven. Stuart Pearce, Des Walker and Nigel Clough featured in both games, but which midfielder (the 1,000th player to be capped by England) played against Chile in May 1989 and which right-back lined up against Malaysia in June 1991?

9 Which Forest goalkeeper can claim the contrasting distinctions of having scored the first own-goal in the history of the Premier League but saved the only one of forty-eight penalties that Southampton's Matt le Tissier failed to score from?

10 A goal that is still talked about among older
supporters was the winning goal against Burnley in
December 1962, which was still being applauded
by the crowd several minutes later. Which Channel
Islander scored after beating five Burnley defenders?

11 Which Forest European Cup winner is the proud
father of a cricketer who has played in more than
one hundred one-day internationals for England?

# Round

# 22

# 'He gets the ball; he scores a goal'

Just the one, mind. Here's a team (OK, so it has two left-backs) of Reds for you to identify, each of whom managed to score a single goal in their Forest careers. A goalie given a gift, defenders in nosebleed territory, and as for the rest – holding a banjo, looking at a barn door and wondering what to do…

I   Who slotted home the fastest ever goal scored by a goalkeeper in professional football in a rescheduled League Cup tie against Leicester City in 2007? The Foxes had sportingly allowed Forest to restore the one-goal advantage we held when the original game was abandoned after Leicester's Clive Clarke suffered a serious heart problem.

2 Which mid-1960s full-back was replaced initially by Henry Newton and, longer-term, by John Winfield?

3 Which defender made his only substitute appearance in more than 500 League games for Newcastle and Forest when he replaced Peter Withe at Ipswich in April 1978, was told by Brian Clough to play up front – and promptly scored the only League goal of his career?

4 The only goal in this Forest legend's club and international career of over 700 appearances came on New Year's Day 1992, when he beat his Forest team-mate Steve Sutton, who was on loan with Luton Town at the time, to score a last-minute equaliser.

5 The one goal this 1970s Northern Irish international
defender managed technically didn't count.
He scored in the FA Cup 6th round in 1974 but
hosts Newcastle's 4–3 win was declared void,
as hundreds of their followers had invaded the pitch
with the Reds 3–1 up against ten men (at least one
Forest player was physically assaulted) and the rest
of the game was played out with both Forest and the
referee fearful of further hooliganism.

6 This non-playing 12th Man at the 1959 FA Cup Final
had a namesake midfielder who played for us in
the 1990s.

7 This French midfielder scored regularly for
Plymouth but just the once for Forest in the
mid-2000s.

8 This striker made his first League appearance for us as a 16 year old in 2001, before having a moderately successful career in the lower leagues.

9 This striker began his career with Forest but made his name as a prolific scorer in two spells with Walsall and as a manager, including three stints in charge of Grimsby.

10 This striker had a lean time on Trentside, having been signed as a replacement for Kevin Campbell, but was a regular scorer for several of his other clubs including Crystal Palace, Barnsley and Wimbledon.

11 This midfielder-cum-striker had a father who won a European Cup medal with Forest and a namesake who once scored a winning goal against the Reds at Wembley.

# 'Nottingham Forest are magic'

…we all agree! Throughout football's history, Forest have been great pioneers and innovators and the club has probably been responsible for, or involved in, more firsts than any other club. Several of them are included in the rounds about the club's early history and elsewhere in this book, but here's a whole round of relatively recent Forest firsts.

I    It's well-known that Forest were the first club to pay a fee of £1 million for a player when we signed Trevor Francis from Birmingham City in 1979. But which club, surprisingly perhaps, were our main competitors for his signature until Brian Clough and Peter Taylor clinched the deal?

2  What was distinctive about the seating in the Executive (now Brian Clough) Stand when it was opened in 1980?

3  Who scored the first ever goal in live TV coverage of a Football League match when he opened the scoring for us at Tottenham in October 1983?

4  Neil Webb became the first visiting player to score on which club's controversial artificial pitch, when he netted on his Forest debut in a 1–1 draw in August 1985?

5  In 1989 Forest became the first club to win two domestic finals at Wembley in the same season. We beat Luton 3–1 in the League Cup but who did we beat 4–3 after extra time in the Simod (Full Members') Cup?

6  Who became the first black player to be transferred for a seven-figure fee when he joined us in 1981?

7  Which Forest player scored the first goal of Sky TV's live coverage of the Premier League in 1992?

8  Forest were the first team to score 7 goals in an away match in the Premier League. Who did we beat 7–1 on April Fool's Day 1995?

9  In which season did Forest become the first European Cup-winning club to be relegated to their country's third tier?

10  What distinction did Amy Fearn achieve at the game between Coventry City and Forest at the Ricoh Arena in February 2010?

11  Which player is believed to have been the first player to win two different clubs' Goal of the Season awards in the same season, with goals against Millwall (for Wolves) and against Leeds (for Forest) in the 2011/12 season?

# 'We're by far the greatest team'

As with all those Forest firsts, there are numerous records throughout this book, but here are a few more records and other achievements of note.

1　Forest share the record for the biggest away win in the League Cup – who were we visiting and what was the score?

2　What is officially Forest's record home attendance?

3  What was the record number of unbeaten top-flight games that Forest set between November 1978 and December 1979?

4  What is Forest's highest-ever points tally in a League season?

5  Who, with 685 games in all competitions between 1951 and 1969, made the most career appearances for Forest?

6  In 2009/10 Forest established a new club record of successive home League wins. This being Forest, during this run we also managed to lose seven away games in a row and put paid to any hopes of automatic promotion, but for how many games did the home-winning run last?

7  Who became the first man to win the FA Cup with three different teams when we beat Luton in the 1959 Final?

8 Forest's highest ever average League attendance was recorded in which season?

9 Who was Forest's first £100,000 signing?

10 Who was the youngest player to turn out in a competitive game for Forest?

11 And who was the oldest?

# 'I was born under a Trent End goal'

In modern times the Trent End has been joined by the A block of the Peter Taylor Stand and, more recently, the lower tier of the Bridgford Stand as the noisiest parts of the ground. Wherever they've gathered, Forest's more vocal fans have come up with their fair share of chants over the years (even the ubiquitous 'Come on you reds/ blues/yellows' may have its origins in chants of 'C'mon you redduns!' in the early 1970s). Meanwhile, supporters young and old have found themselves at the mercy of the latest marketing trends or grown men in comedy costumes.

1  In 1977, Brian Clough reacted to the language used in some Trent End songs by displaying a sign reading 'Gentlemen, no swearing, please! Brian' at a subsequent game. When Clough was interviewed for the England manager's job, the fans displayed a sign of their own – what did it say?

2  At which match did fans display a banner reading, 'Robbo makes Phil Kneel'?

3  Forest supporters produced a number of printed fanzines over the years. What were the names of the first and last ones to be widely available, and the one whose related online forum is still going strong?

4  On what occasion did the Trent End famously chant, 'Two goals are enough, tra-la-la-la-la'?

5  In the late 1980s there was a terrace craze for inflatables, with blow-up bananas being particularly popular. What Forest-related inflatable was seen at the City Ground and Wembley around this time?

6  Opposition fans' taunts of 'You're not famous any more' are usually met with a chorus of 'You're not famous anyway'. What further riposte do Forest fans then give if the Reds score first?

7  When have Forest fans 'never felt more like singing the blues'?

8  Which cult hero midfielder is the subject of a version of 'Yellow Submarine', which lists a full team line-up with this player in every position?

9  In various of Forest's relegation seasons,
the long-suffering fans have been the subject of
taunts of 'Going down, going down, going down'
from opposition fans. What has the reply been on
several occasions when the other team has also
been in trouble near the foot of the table?

10  Which chant was recorded in the Trent End and
used for the introduction of the 'We've Got the
Whole World in Our Hands' single?

11  Name the three mascots Forest have used to
entertain younger fans in recent years – and which
one was briefly kidnapped in September 2004?

# 'Shall we sing a song for you?'

The club's links with the music scene have been many and varied over the years. Whether it's players forming bands, fans lauding players or ill-advised attempts at chart domination, the club has a music-related heritage (calling it a 'musical heritage' would test the definition of the word 'musical', in many cases) that must surely match that of many higher-profile clubs. Who knew that the City Ground was such a musical hotbed?

1  Which TV theme tune did Forest run out to at the City Ground for several decades, beginning in 1956?

2  In 1978, which Nottingham pop group accompanied the Reds' players in their cover of 'We've Got the Whole World in Our Hands', which reached number 24 in the charts, an unusually high position for a football record?

3  What was the record label the Stranglers named after a Red who was one of their biggest fans?

4  The name of which song by Irish band The Sultans of Ping FC was taken from a Brian Clough quotation about John Robertson?

5  Two youngsters who briefly made the Forest first team in the 1990s went on to have careers in music. Which striker put together Britpop band Merc and post-punk group Ulterior, and which midfielder formed The Establishment and persuaded Stuart Pearce, Des Walker and Teddy Sheringham to appear in the video for their debut single?

6  Which old standard was covered by Peter Shilton and Ray Clemence in 1980, at a time when England manager Ron Greenwood had a curious policy of selecting England's best keeper and Clemence for alternate games?

7 Which troubled Forest forward released a single called 'Do It 'Cos You Like It' in 1982?

8 Which Forest fans' battle cry was used as the title of a compilation of Forest-related songs issued by Cherry Red Records in 1996?

9 Who is the only Forest player to feature in the song lyrics of humorous indie social commentators Half Man Half Biscuit?

10 Which Forest legend made an appearance in the Sausage Sandwich game on Danny Baker's show on Radio 5 Live, in which he impersonated Brian Clough performing AC/DC's 'A Whole Lotta Rosie'?

11 Which world-famous pop musician is a close relative of Roy Dwight?

# 'You'll never sing this'

Champions of Europe – you'll never sing this, as we like to remind our friends from the wrong end of the Brian Clough Way, to whom we dedicate this round. Intense as the rivalry between Forest and Derby is, it is largely based on the last fifty years or so. In this period the clubs' often contrasting fortunes have frequently been influenced by the numerous players and managers they have in common, epitomised by both clubs winning the League under the management of Brian Clough and Peter Taylor. There must have been a certain amount of needle between the clubs before then, though, as a match between the teams in 1896 was abandoned after the crowd invaded the pitch, while eighteen months later they met in the 1898 FA Cup Final. And we all know what happened then …

1  In 1974/75, Derby's most recent Championship-winning season, their average home League attendance was 26,719. What was Forest's in our own title-winning season just three years later?

2  In Derby's last spell in Division 3 (from 1984 to 1986) they averaged 11,610. What was Forest's average League attendance in our last spell in the third tier from 2005 to 2008?

3  How many major trophies have the East Midlands' biggest club and Derby each won?

4  What are Forest's and Derby's highest ever placings in the Premier League?

5  Which trophy is played for every time Forest and Derby County meet in a competitive match or even a friendly?

6  Forest's two biggest wins against Derby both came in the same season, 1903/04. What were the scores that gave Forest a double over their local rivals with an aggregate of 11–3?

7  Seven of Derby's 1971/72 Championship-winning squad also played for Forest, either before or after their time with the Rams. Name them.

8  A photo of Derby's goalkeeper apparently bowing in obeisance to a Forest striker in our 3–0 win early in the 1977/78 Championship-winning season later appeared regularly on the Forest programme cover. Who were the players in question?

9  Who blasted Forest into a first-minute lead in the 3–2 win over the Rams in August 2009 that was remembered for Nathan Tyson's post-match celebrations with a corner flag?

10  After Forest thrashed Derby 5–2 on 29 December 2010 Reds fans referred to the Brian Clough Way as the A 5–2. Which two former Rams both scored twice?

11  'Who put the ball in the Derby net' in the last minute at the iPro Stadium to give struggling Forest an unexpected 2–1 win on 17 January 2015?

# 'Oh mist rolling in from the Trent'

Not only can Forest boast arguably the best badge in English football, but a strong case can be made that we have the best-located ground in the country too. The River Trent is so close that a match was once postponed when the pitch was perfectly playable but the embankment flooded to within a few yards of the back of the Trent End, while in the other direction one of the world's best-loved Test match grounds is visible from the Brian Clough Stand. What's more, the City Ground is a proper, atmospheric football ground that has evolved over more than a century and not some soul-less identikit stadium on an anonymous industrial estate.

1   In which year did Forest move to the City Ground?

2 Why is it called the City Ground, despite being on the south side of the Trent and therefore in the county of Nottinghamshire?

3 In 1946/47, when winter floods left the City Ground under water to within a couple of feet of the crossbars (and destroyed many of the club's records and archives), on what date did the season finally end for Forest?

4 On how many occasions has the City Ground been used for an FA Cup semi-final or replay?

5 On 24 August 1968, a Forest home game was abandoned at half time after a fire broke out in the Main Stand, mercifully without loss of life. *Goal* magazine had previewed the game with a headline claiming the opposition were 'ready to set fire to Forest', while the previous week 'Fire' by the Crazy World of Arthur Brown had been at number one in the UK charts. Who were our opponents that day?

6  What was the popular name of the cartoon figure with the star-shaped head in the Shipstone's advertisement on the old scoreboard at the back of the Bridgford End?

7  In February 1977, the mist rolling in from the Trent played a significant part in the Reds' promotion bid. It caused a match to be abandoned when we were a goal down and heading for a third successive defeat. When the game was replayed we won 2–1 and the two points helped us go up in third place. Who were our opponents?

8  Which three countries contested Group D matches at the City Ground during Euro 96?

9  In April 2002, a City Ground crowd of almost 30,000 watched the Heineken Cup semi-final between which two rugby union teams?

10  Which major rock group played in front of a 20,000
    crowd at the City Ground during their 2005
    world tour?

11  The previous highest crowd for this fixture had
    been less than 14,000, but the City Ground hosted
    crowds of more than 24,000 for it in both 2007 and
    2008. What was the fixture?

# Round

# 29

# 'Who are ya? Who are ya?'

We all like to try and recall line-ups from the past, so here are the starting elevens for some significant games from Forest's history, but with one name missing from each. They are listed in traditional fashion, from 1 to 11. Who are the mystery players?

## 1 FA Cup Final win v Derby, 1898

Alsop

| Richie | ? | McPherson | Scott |
| McInnes | Wragg | Richards | Spouncer |
| | Capes | Benbow | |

## 2 FA Cup Final win v Luton, 1959

Thomson

| Whare | McKinlay | Burkitt | McDonald |
| Dwight | Quigley | ? | Imlach |
| | Gray | Wilson | |

### 3  FA Cup 6th round win v Everton, 1967

Grummitt
Hindley    McKinlay    Hennessey    Winfield
Lyons    **?**    Newton    Storey-Moore
Wignall    Baker

### 4  Abandoned FA Cup 6th round tie v Newcastle, 1974

Barron
O'Kane    Chapman    Serella    Winfield
O'Neill    Lyall    **?**    Bowyer
Martin    McKenzie

### 5  Final game of 1976–77 promotion season v Millwall

**?**
Anderson    Chapman    Lloyd    Clark
O'Neill    McGovern    Bowyer    Robertson
Withe    Woodcock

### 6  League Cup Final replay win v Liverpool, 1978

|          |          | Woods    |           |
|----------|----------|----------|-----------|
| Anderson | Burns    | Lloyd    | Clark     |
| O'Neill  | ?        | Bowyer   | Robertson |
|          | Withe    | Woodcock |           |

### 7  European Cup Final win v Malmö, 1979

|          |          | Shilton  |           |
|----------|----------|----------|-----------|
| Anderson | Burns    | Lloyd    | Clark     |
| Francis  | McGovern | Bowyer   | Robertson |
|          | ?        | Robertson |          |

### 8  European Cup Final win v Hamburg, 1980

|   |          |          | Shilton |           |
|---|----------|----------|---------|-----------|
|   | Anderson | Burns    | Lloyd   | Gray      |
| ? | O'Neill  | McGovern | Bowyer  | Robertson |
|   |          | Birtles  |         |           |

### 9 League Cup win v Luton, 1989

Sutton

| Laws | Wilson | Walker | Pearce |
|------|--------|--------|--------|
| Gaynor | Webb | ? | Parker |
| | Clough | Chapman | |

### 10 FA Cup Final defeat v Tottenham, 1991

Crossley

| Charles | Chettle | Walker | Pearce |
|---------|---------|--------|--------|
| Crosby | Keane | Parker | ? |
| | Clough | Glover | |

### 11 Promotion-clinching win v Yeovil, 2008

Smith

| Chambers | Wilson | Morgan | Bennett |
|----------|--------|--------|---------|
| Commons | Perch | McGugan | ? |
| | Ormerod | Tyson | |

## Round

# 30

# 'You what? You what? You what, you what, you what?'

Finally, like reserve players being given a run-out at the end of the season, here are a few more odds and ends that didn't quite make it into the rest of the quiz.

1  In the years after the Second World War, 'Jack' was in the habit of boarding a trolley-bus in the Old Market Square and joining the supporters travelling to Trent Bridge for Forest home games. Who or what was Jack?

2  Who led the Forest team out at Wembley for the 1980 League Cup Final against Wolves?

3   What was the headline in the *Evening Post* in 1996 which wrongly suggested Forest were looking to sign an Italian superstar to replace Stan Collymore and has since become a watchword among Forest fans for improbable media speculation about transfer targets?

4   Which 1990s Forest forward's hairstyle prompted chants of 'He's got a pineapple on his head' from the opposition's fans?

5   Which five players have scored more than a hundred League goals for the Reds?

6   *Nottingham Forest* was withdrawn from service in 1960, the year in which *Notts Forest* was constructed. What were they?

7   Forest were the only away team to win at Old Trafford in the 1994/95 Premier League season. What percentage of the goals Manchester United conceded at home that season did we score?

8   Who are the only three players to feature in lists of both the top ten appearances and the top ten goal scorers in competitive games for Forest?

9   Which Forest player has the distinction of having scored the last ever goal recorded on BBC TV's Ceefax football pages?

10  Who became Forest's first ever substitute when he replaced Colin Addison in the 2–1 defeat at Leeds in September 1965?

11  Who was the last Forest player to score in a Cup Final win?

THE ANSWERS

1  1865.
2  Shinney (also known as shinty).
3  The Clinton Arms.
4  The club first played at The Forest recreation ground (and is thus only indirectly named after Sherwood Forest).
5  Walter Lymbery.
6  Tinsley Lindley.
7  Sam Widdowson.
8  2–3–5.
9  A whistle – prior to that, flags had been used.
10  Notts County.
11  Queen's Park.

# 'Down through history'

1 Arsenal.
2 Goal nets.
3 Clapton; 14–0.
4 The Football Alliance.
5 Everton (2–2, away); Derby County (3–2, away).
6 The Crystal Palace.
7 Arthur Capes (2) and John McPherson.
8 The team were in white shirts, as the photographer was apparently concerned that Forest's red would not reproduce well in black and white.
9 Argentina and Uruguay.
10 The Argentinian team Independiente.
11 Leicester Fosse; 12–0.

# 'We will follow the Forest'

1  £50 plus £10 a week for the rest of the season.
2  Everton.
3  Newcastle United.
4  Injured earlier in the game, Martin was helped back onto the field (presumably by team-mates too scared to take the kick themselves) to score past England international goalkeeper Dick Pym and rescue a point for the Reds.
5  Tommy Graham.
6  The Netherlands.
7  Greyhound racing.
8  He scored from inside his own half – his only goal in well over 200 appearances for the Reds.
9  Barnsley.
10  Swansea Town.
11  Bombs.

## Round 4 'On to victory'

1 70; 110; 36 (Wally Ardron).
2 Sheffield Wednesday.
3 7–1.
4 Brian Clough and Peter Taylor.
5 Sheffield United.
6 It was Manchester United's first League game after the Munich air disaster, played the day after Duncan Edwards became the eighth United player to die as a result of the crash.
7 Tooting & Mitcham United.
8 Tommy Wilson.
9 The lap of honour with the trophy.
10 Wednesbury.
11 St Mirren.

**Round 5** **'Nottingham, Nottingham, Nottingham'**

1  17.
2  Trent Bridge.
3  1900/01 – County finished 3rd and Forest a point behind in 4th.
4  Iremonger.
5  J.B. Priestley. His memories of the game were not the clearest, however. Despite referring to 'the County' scoring a goal, from the date of his journey the game in question would have been one which Forest actually won 2–0.
6  None.
7  1950/51.
8  1975/76 (County finished 5th in Division 2 with 49 points, Forest 8th with 46).
9  *Saturday Afternoon and Sunday Morning.*
10  Wes Morgan.
11  David Johnson.

1  Tommy Cavanagh.
2  Bobby McKinlay.
3  Stoke City.
4  Chris Crowe.
5  Swindon Town.
6  *Quiz Ball*. Forest lost 3–2 after 'extra time'.
7  Brian Labone.
8  Frank Wignall.
9  Terry Hennessey.
10  Nine.
11  The Football Writers' Footballer of the Year award.

# 'Off! Off! Off!'

1  Thirty-two years (1939 to 1971).
2  The aforementioned Sammy Chapman, against Leeds (1971), Norwich (1974) and Fulham (1975).
3  Just twice – against Leicester City in a League Cup tie in 1989 and Tottenham in a League game two years later.
4  Stan Collymore.
5  David Platt.
6  Wolverhampton Wanderers.
7  David Prutton, with five red cards between 2000 and 2007.
8  Coventry City.
9  Michael Dawson.
10  Guy Moussi.
11  The 2011 play-off semi-final first leg at home to Swansea City (we went on to lose the second leg 3–1).

# 'We're going to Grimsby'

1 Derby County won the title, managed by a certain Brian Clough and Peter Taylor.
2 41.
3 Just 6 – and 3 of Campbell's came on the opening day at Coventry.
4 Alan Fettis.
5 Colin Cooper and Kevin Campbell.
6 30. Still, it was 19 more than Derby managed in 2007/08.
7 He went to the wrong dug-out (and wondered why a team with such good substitutes was bottom of the league).
8 Chris Bart-Williams.
9 Marlon King.
10 Mick Harford.
11 Plymouth Argyle.

# Round 9 'Brian Clough and Peter Taylor!'

1 Bert Bowery, for £2,000 from Worksop Town.
2 Neil Martin.
3 The 1979 League Cup Final against Southampton.
4 *With Clough by Taylor.*
5 'The goods round the back.'
6 Laughter.
7 Sheffield United.
8 Nigel Clough, appropriately enough.
9 *In the Spirit of the Man.*
10 £70,000 (smashing the original target of £60,000).
11 The People's Run.

# 'And now you're gonna believe us'

1  Jim Barrett.
2  14; they drew 2–2 and finished a point behind us with a much worse goal difference.
3  U-Win.
4  Carlisle United, Sheffield United and Burnley.
5  Millwall.
6  Steve Chettle.
7  Stan Collymore (2) and Stuart Pearce.
8  Frank Clark.
9  Chris Bart-Williams.
10  Marlon Harewood.
11  Van Hooijdonk scored 29 and Campbell 23.

# 'You what?'

1 Stewart Imlach, *My Father and Other Working-Class Football Heroes* by Gary Imlach.
2 Kilmarnock and Ayr United.
3 Matt Gillies (the players were Terry Hennessey, Henry Newton, Ian Storey-Moore and Peter Cormack, all sold between February 1970 and July 1972).
4 It was an England squad, manager Don Revie and his staff not having realised Robertson was a Scot.
5 Peter Grummitt.
6 Gary Crosby.
7 He accidentally knocked out the linesman as he ran along the touchline whirling his arm in delight.
8 The Forman brothers – Frank (1 goal) and Fred (2 goals).
9 Andrew Marriott.
10 Ian Storey-Moore.
11 Wally Ardron.

# 'The best damn team in the land'

1   Everton 1 Forest 3.
2   Peter Withe.
3   Manchester United, 4–0.
4   Coventry City's Highfield Road.
5   7 (in the days of 2 points for a win).
6   24.
7   23.
8   +45 (69 for, 24 against).
9   Peter Shilton.
10  Tony Woodcock.
11  Kenny Burns.

# 'Running round Wembley with the Cup'

1  All yellow.
2  Kenny Burns.
3  23 (5 v West Ham, 4 v both Notts County and Aston Villa, 3 against Bury and 7 over two legs against Leeds United).
4  Chris Woods.
5  Four – he scored twice and had two more 'goals' disallowed for offside.
6  *Yesterday's Hero*.
7  Nigel Clough.
8  Lee Chapman.
9  Tommy Gaynor, who won the Irish League Cup with Cork City in 1995.
10  The release from prison of Nelson Mandela.
11  Nigel Jemson.

# 'We've won the Cup twice!'

1  Garry Birtles.
2  Ten days short of his 17th birthday, he became the youngest ever player in the European Cup.
3  John Robertson.
4  Trevor Francis.
5  Just four – three in the League and the FA Cup 5th round tie against Arsenal.
6  Ajax.
7  Frank Gray (he played for Leeds in the 1975 final).
8  Kevin Keegan (though it should, of course, have been John Robertson).
9  In his excitement he blurted out, 'And Hamburg are champions of Europe again!'
10  22 years – so how come Ferguson got a knighthood and not Clough?
11  Frank Gray, Bryn Gunn and John O'Hare.

# 'We'll support you ever more!'

**1** Fourteen – the last eight matches of 1912/13 and the first six of 1913/14.

**2** Blackburn Rovers 9 Forest 1 (and Rovers were actually responsible for all ten goals, as our goal was an own-goal).

**3** It was Blackburn again – and they beat us 7–0, with ex-Red Lars Bohinen scoring twice.

**4** Nineteen.

**5** Ole Gunnar Solskjær.

**6** Sheffield United (2003), Yeovil Town (2007), Blackpool (2010) and Swansea City (2011).

**7** Paul Hart and Steve Cotterill.

**8** The ball bounced off a stray, wind-blown takeaway coffee cup just as Forest keeper Barry Roche was about to kick it clear, leaving Paul Peschisolido with a simple tap-in. Forest fans claimed it at least gave Derby a cup to display in their trophy cabinet.

**9** Woking.

**10** Weymouth and Salisbury City.

**11** Chester City.

# 'To Europe, to Europe'

1 Billy Cobb (*v* Valencia in the Fairs Cup in 1961/62).
2 Steve Stone (*v* Bayern Munich in the UEFA Cup in 1995/96).
3 Malmö – we were 5–1 up when the match was abandoned because of fog.
4 Valencia, Forest's first opponents in European competition four years earlier.
5 Joe Baker.
6 Having won 2–1 at home but lost 1–0 away, the Forest players waited patiently for extra-time to begin, only to find their opponents celebrating, as we had apparently not been aware that the 'away goals' rule counted after ninety minutes of the 2nd leg and not after extra time. Whoops.
7 Steve Hodge and Colin Walsh.
8 Anderlecht, who, happily, went on to lose on penalties to Tottenham Hotspur in the final.
9 Three – Forest finished third in the League in both 1988 and 1989, and won the League Cup in both 1989 and 1990, any of which would have ensured qualification for the UEFA Cup.
10 1995/96.
11 Ian Bowyer.

# 'He's gonna cry in a minute'

1  We weren't drawn at home at all in either campaign.
2  Calvin Plummer.
3  Nigel Clough.
4  None. We won 3–0, 2–0, 3–0 and 1–0 in the first four rounds.
5  John Aldridge.
6  Neil Webb.
7  Nigel Jemson.
8  Colin Foster.
9  The World's Greatest Grandad.
10  Garry Parker and Gary Charles.
11  Roger Milford.

# 'Psycho, Psycho, Psycho!'

1 Ian Butterworth.

2 Electrician.

3 16, an English record for a defender.

4 A life-size cardboard cut-out of him.

5 76 (by far a club record).

6 Newcastle United, the manager in question being Kevin Keegan.

7 He picked a team that he thought might give us a decent chance of a win – but his wife pointed out that his eleven did not include a goalkeeper.

8 'Screaming' – in delight, relief and who knows how many other emotions, after scoring his penalty in the shoot-out against Spain at Euro 96, having returned to the side a year after losing his place to an inferior replacement.

9 'Forest red'.

10 Blackpool (we won 2–0).

11 '... the carrot ...'

# 'He's one of our own'

1  Darren Ward.
2  Viv Anderson.
3  Julian Bennett.
4  Steve Chettle.
5  'Big Wes' Morgan. A fan congratulated him on his on 400th appearance for the Reds and the bemused owner of the handle, Wesley Hall, soon became one of what he calls the 'Forest family', visiting the City Ground for the first time in October 2015.
6  Henry Newton.
7  Darren Huckerby.
8  Jermaine Jenas.
9  Garry Birtles.
10  Tony Woodcock.
11  Steve Hodge.

1 217.
2 Tom Peacock (against Barnsley, Port Vale and Doncaster Rovers).
3 Dave 'Boy' Martin.
4 Wally Ardron.
5 Roy Dwight.
6 26.
7 Archie Gemmill, *v* Arsenal in 1977/78.
8 Tommy Gemmell (1967 and 1970 for Celtic),
   Peter Withe (1982 for Aston Villa) and
   Teddy Sheringham (1999 for Manchester United).
9 Neil Webb and Garry Birtles.
10 Jack Lester.
11 Garath McCleary, in the bizarre 7–3 win at Leeds United in March 2012.

# 'You what? You what?'

1  Tinsley Lindley, Frank Forman, Peter Shilton and Stuart Pearce.
2  Kenny Burns.
3  Gary Megson.
4  Ian Storey-Moore and Henry Newton.
5  David Frost.
6  Panasonic (1981–83).
7  Billy Sharp.
8  Neil Webb; Gary Charles.
9  Mark Crossley.
10 Dick 'Flip' le Flem.
11 Bryn Gunn, whose daughter Jenny also played in eleven Test matches.

# 'He gets the ball; he scores a goal'

1  Paul Smith.
2  Dennis Mochan.
3  Frank Clark.
4  Des Walker.
5  Liam O'Kane.
6  Geoff Thomas.
7  David Friio.
8  Craig Westcarr.
9  Alan Buckley.
10  Neil Shipperley.
11  Andy Gray.

1  Coventry City.
2  It was the first time a club's name had been picked out in seats of a contrasting colour.
3  Colin Walsh.
4  Luton Town.
5  Everton.
6  Justin Fashanu.
7  Teddy Sheringham, in a 1–0 win against Liverpool.
8  Sheffield Wednesday.
9  2004/05.
10 She became the first woman to referee a Football League match when, as the senior assistant referee, she took control of the last twenty minutes after referee Tony Bates suffered a calf strain.
11 Adlene Guedioura.

# 'We're by far the greatest team'

1 8–0 v Doncaster Rovers (11 August 1987).

2 49,946 v Manchester United on 28 October 1967 ('officially' because some accounts talk of the actual figure exceeding 50,000 due to some fans getting in without paying).

3 42 – the equivalent of an entire season unbeaten. Arsenal's 'Invincibles' beat Forest's record in October 2004, though they used 33 players in their eventual 49-game run, whereas we fielded just 18.

4 94 in Division 1, 1997/98.

5 Bobby McKinlay.

6 12.

7 Billy Walker – as a player with Aston Villa in 1920 and as a manager with Sheffield Wednesday in 1935 and then Forest.

8 1967/68 – 33,775.

9 Jim Baxter, for £105,000 from Sunderland in December 1967.

10 Steve Burke (16 years, 22 days, v Ayr United, Anglo-Scottish Cup, 1976/77).

11 Dave Beasant (42 years, 47 days, v Tranmere Rovers, Division 1, 2000/01)

1   'Brian, no leaving please! The Gentlemen'.

2   The 1978 League Cup Final v Liverpool.

3   *(The Almighty) Brian; Blooming Forest; Lost That Lovin' Feeling.*

4   When Colin Barrett made it 2–0 at the end of the first leg of our European Cup tie against Liverpool in September 1978 – the visiting Liverpool fans had been chanting, 'One goal's not enough, tra-la-la-la-la'.

5   An inflatable 'tricky tree', i.e. the iconic Forest badge in blow–up form.

6   'One–nil to the famous team'.

7   'When Forest win and Derby lose', though that scenario shouldn't really give Forest fans the blues at all!

8   Brian Rice – the chorus that follows is 'We all live in a world of Brian Rice'.

9   'So are we, so are we, so are we…'

10   'Nottingham Forest are magic, we all agree, Nottingham Forest are magic, are magic, are magic…'

11   Nutty the Squirrel, Sherwood Bear (the kidnapping victim) and Robin Hood. Sherwood was reinstated as mascot before the 2015/16 season.

# 'Shall we sing a song for you?'

1 Dick James' recording of the *Robin Hood* theme.
2 Paper Lace.
3 Psycho.
4 'Give Him a Ball And a Yard of Grass'.
5 Paul McGregor; John Burns.
6 'Side By Side'. It didn't bother the charts.
7 Justin Fashanu.
8 *You Reds!*
9 Peter Grummitt, who gets a somewhat surreal name-check in the song 'Let's Not'.
10 John McGovern.
11 Elton John, who was born Reginald Kenneth Dwight and is variously said to be Roy's cousin or his nephew – he is the former, according to Elton's own website.

# 'You'll never sing this'

1 32,501.
2 20,277.
3 Forest – 9 (1 League title, 2 FA Cups, 4 League Cups and 2 European Cups); Derby – 3 (2 League titles, 1 FA Cup).
4 Forest – 3rd (in 1995), Derby 8th (in 1999).
5 The Brian Clough Trophy.
6 Derby 2 Forest 6 and Forest 5 Derby 1.
7 Archie Gemmill, Terry Hennessey, Alan Hinton, John McGovern, John O'Hare, Colin Todd and Frank Wignall.
8 The Derby keeper was Colin Boulton and the Forest forward was Peter Withe.
9 Radi Majewski.
10 Marcus Tudgay and Rob Earnshaw.
11 Derby-born Ben Osborn.

# 'Oh mist rolling in from the Trent'

1  1898.
2  Nottingham had been granted city status in 1897 and the ground was at the time within the city boundaries.
3  14 June.
4  Five – in 1901, 1902, 1905, 1961 and 1965.
5  Leeds United.
6  Ivor Thirst.
7  Southampton.
8  Croatia, Portugal and Turkey.
9  Leicester and Llanelli – the Tigers won 13–12.
10  REM.
11  The FA Women's Cup Final.

# 'Who are ya?
# Who are ya?'

1 Frank Forman.
2 Jeff Whitefoot.
3 John Barnwell.
4 John Robertson.
5 John Middleton.
6 John O'Hare.
7 Garry Birtles.
8 Gary Mills.
9 Steve Hodge.
10 Ian Woan.
11 Chris Cohen.

# 'You what? You what? You what, you what, you what?'

I   A jackdaw, whose presence was, unfortunately for him, noticed at one too many games the Reds lost, which eventually led to a fatal encounter with a superstitious supporter's shotgun.

2   Coach Jimmy Gordon.

3   'It's Baggio!'

4   Jason Lee.

5   Grenville Morris (199), Wally Ardron (123), Johnny Dent (119), Ian Storey-Moore (105) and Nigel Clough (102).

6   A railway engine (built in 1937) and an ignorantly named trawler (scrapped in 1991).

7   50 per cent – our 2–1 win accounted for half of the 4 goals United let in.

8   Grenville Morris, Ian Bowyer and John Robertson.

9   Dexter Blackstock, who scored a last-minute equaliser for the Reds at Blackpool on 23 October 2012, the last day of analogue TV in the UK.

10  Barry McArthur.

11  Scot Gemmill, who scored the winning goal in extra time against Southampton in the 1992 ZDS (Full Members') Cup at Wembley.

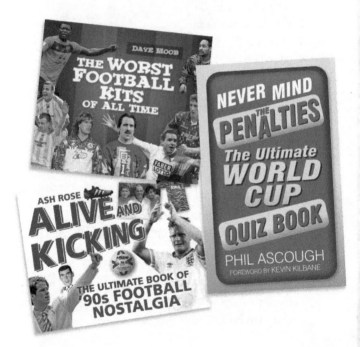